FORMS OF GOVERNMENT: NEED TO KNOW

DICTATORSHIP

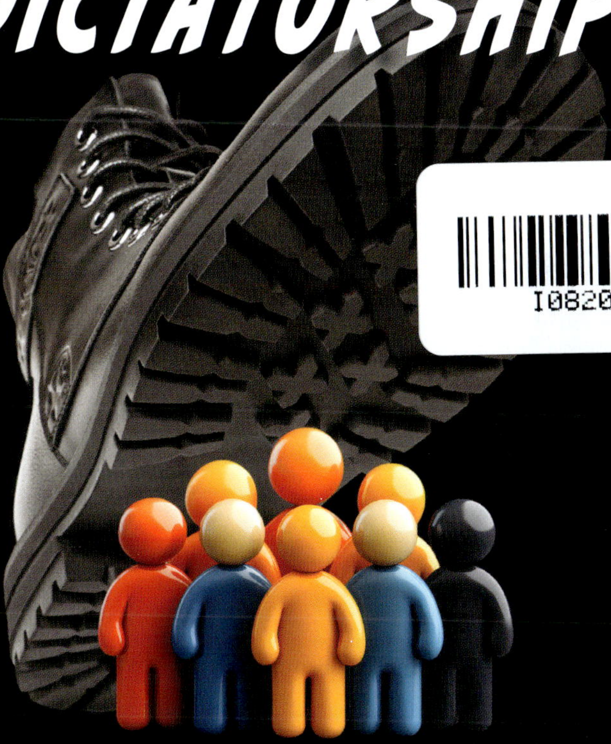

by D. R. Faust

Consultant: Caitlin Krieck, Social Studies Teacher and Instructional Coach, The Lab School of Washington

SilverTip Books, an imprint of Bearport Publishing by FlutterBee

Credits
Cover and title page, © SlayStorm/Shutterstock and © MDT/Adobe Stock; 3, © PeskyMonkey/Shutterstock; 4–5, © MangoStar_Studio/iStock; 7, © Robson90/Shutterstock; 8–9, © zef art/Shutterstock; 11, © zakir1346/Shutterstock; 12–13, © Shawshots/Alamy Stock Photo; 15, © Gil Corzo/Shutterstock; 17, © Anadolu/Getty Images; 18, © ART Collection/Alamy Stock Photo; 19, © Album/Alamy Stock Photo; 21, © Shawshots/Alamy Stock Photo; 23, © Archivart/Alamy Stock Photo; 25, © North Korea Picture Library/Alamy Stock Photo; 27, © Jose Calsina/Shutterstock.

Bearport Publishing Company Product Development Team
Kayla Eggert, Theresa Emminizer, Kim Jones, Allison Juda, Cole Nelson, Naomi Reich, Steve Scheluchin, Tiana Tran

Statement on Usage of Generative Artificial Intelligence
Bearport Publishing remains committed to publishing high-quality nonfiction books. Therefore, we restrict the use of generative AI to ensure accuracy of all text and visual components pertaining to a book's subject. See BearportPublishing.com for details.

Library of Congress Cataloging-in-Publication Data is available at www.loc.gov or upon request from the publisher.

ISBN: 979-8-89577-636-0 (hardcover)
ISBN: 979-8-89577-790-9 (paperback)
ISBN: 979-8-89577-724-4 (ebook)

For more information, write to Bearport Publishing, 3500 American Blvd W, Suite 150, Bloomington, MN 55431. Printed in the United States of America.

Contents

From Fiction to Reality

Many of our favorite fictional stories feature rulers with total power. This makes for exciting books and movies. It is fun to play against these characters in video games. But this is also a real kind of government called a dictatorship.

There have been many forms of government throughout history. Some have disappeared. Others are still around. Dictatorships have been a form of government for a long time.

Unlimited Power

A dictatorship is a type of **autocracy**. This is a political system where one person holds the majority of the power.

In a dictatorship, the leader is called a dictator. This ruler sometimes shares their power with a few people who are loyal to them. However, average **citizens** do not have any say or choice.

The word *dictator* was first used in ancient Rome. During times of war, the Romans would make someone dictator. This title gave the ruler unlimited power. But it lasted for only a short time.

Julius Caesar was dictator of Rome several times.

Leaders in some forms of government have limits to their powers. But not for a dictator. There is no one to stop them. A dictator makes the laws. They also decide if someone breaks the rules. Some even break their own laws. They do what they want.

Some other forms of government divide responsibilities. Different parts of the government have specific roles. This is called separation of powers.

Don't Tell Me What to Do!

Not all dictatorships are the same. Different dictators may have power over different things.

Sometimes, people under a dictatorship have a few personal freedoms. For example, people may be able to pick their own jobs.

Most dictators want full control. But it is difficult to keep this kind of power. Giving people a small amount of choice may make them easier to rule.

Some dictators rule over every part of life. This is a **totalitarian** (toh-*tal*-i-TAIR-ree-uhn) system. There is often more force used in these governments. The dictators control what students can learn. They may even say how people can dress.

Germany had a totalitarian government under Adolf Hitler. Joseph Stalin controlled the Soviet Union in this way, too.

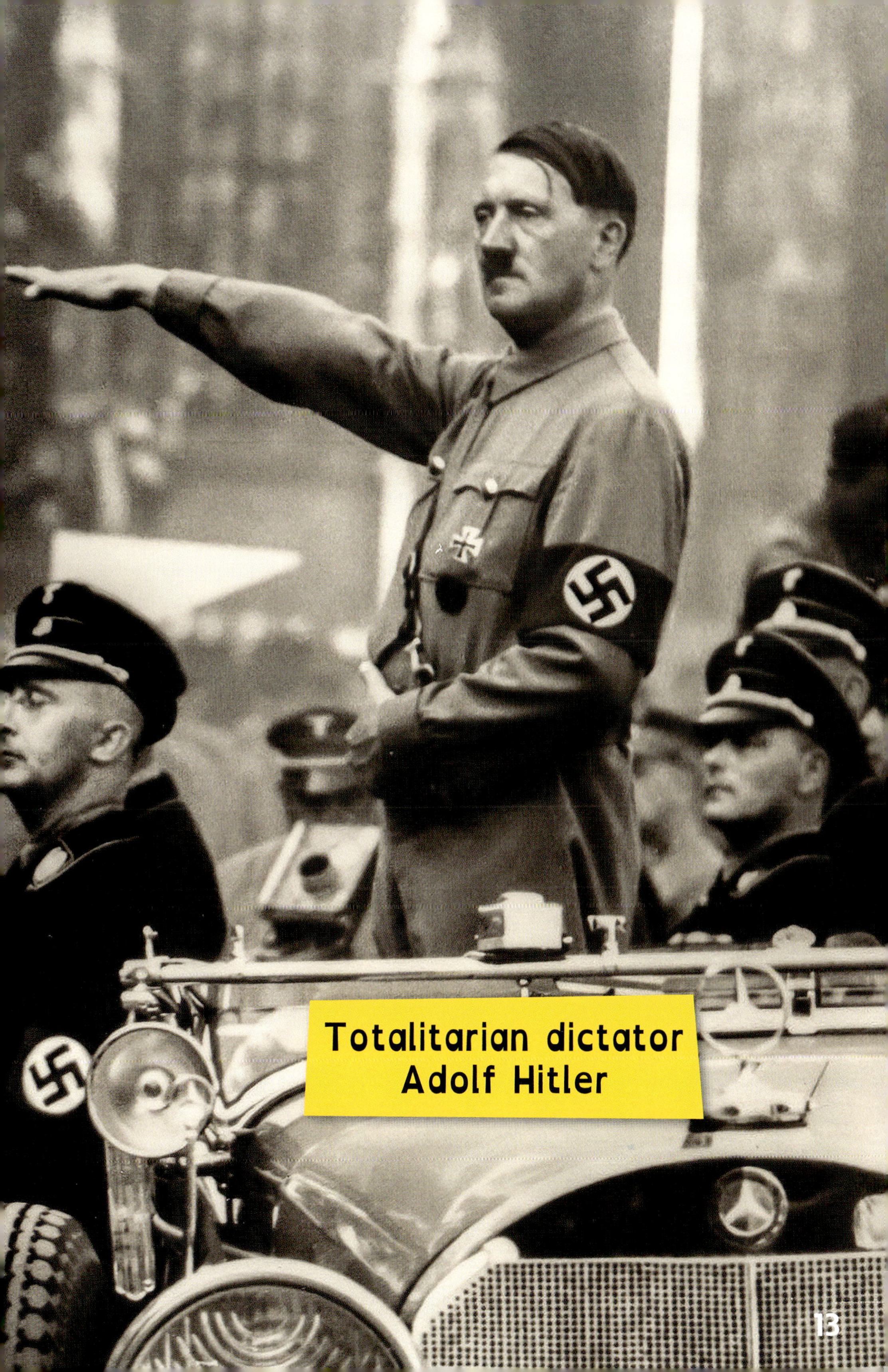

Totalitarian dictator
Adolf Hitler

Taking out the Competition

Dictators can come to power in different ways. Some are elected at first. They slowly take over more control. Then, they strip away power from others. They might ban political parties other than their own. This stops competition in future elections.

A country with only one political party is called a one-party state. China, Cuba, and North Korea are all one-party states.

Xi Jinping is the leader of the only political party in China.

Military Might

Sometimes, a small group may not like the leader of their government. They use force to get rid of this person. Then, they take power themselves. This is called a **coup** (KOO).

Many coups use the power of the military. This makes them hard to stop. It also helps the new leaders keep power.

A revolution can also take over a government. But this is usually led by a large group of citizens. A coup is led by a smaller group from the military.

There was a coup in Niger in July 2023.

Coups may lead to military dictatorships. This is when people from the military run the government. Often, military dictatorships are run by groups. But sometimes, a single leader takes full power. They rule alone.

Throughout history, Japan has been run by several military dictatorships. One of these lasted from 1192 until 1867. During this time, the dictator was called the shogun.

Military officer Augusto Pinochet was the dictator of Chile.

All About the Personality

Most dictators keep control through force or fear. But some create a **cult of personality**. They stay in power by making themselves look good. This often includes lies to make the citizens see them as heroic. These leaders may tell their people that they are the only ones fit to rule.

Dictators control art and the media. They spread targeted stories about themselves and their enemies. This is called **propaganda**.

Propaganda for
Joseph Stalin
С НОВЫМ ГОДОМ,
ЛЮБИМЫЙ СТАЛИН!

Family Ties

In some ways, a **monarchy** is similar to a dictatorship. It is another form of autocracy. This government is led by a single ruler called a monarch.

The difference between this and a dictatorship is simple. Monarchs are always run through family lines.

King Louis XIV of France was a monarch. He ruled from 1643 to 1715. Louis XIV called himself the Sun King. He believed he was the center of French society.

King Louis XIV of France

Still, some dictatorships maintain family ties. Many dictators give important jobs to members of their family. They may give special treatment to businesses run by relatives. When a dictator dies, political power sometimes passes to someone from their family.

When a family rules over a long period, it is called a **dynasty**. This can happen in dictatorships as well as monarchies. The pharaohs of ancient Egypt ruled in dynasties. So did past emperors of China.

North Korea has long been ruled by the Kim family.

Dictatorships in the Digital Age

Dictatorships have changed over time. Leaders have come and gone. And they have held different amounts of control.

Today, social media is reshaping governments everywhere. It is connecting more people faster. Dictatorships and other forms of governments have continued to change to keep up.

As dictatorships change, they may include pieces from different forms of government. In fact, there are few governments around the world that do not have a blend of forms.

Forms of Autocracy

Dictatorships are types of autocracies. They can work several ways.

AUTOCRACIES

Political systems with one person in power

TYPES OF AUTOCRACIES

Dictatorships	Monarchies
Power is held by a single person or small group. Power can be gained and held in a number of ways.	Power is held by a single member from a royal family. Rule is passed down through families.

HOLDING OR KEEPING POWER

One-Party State	Military Dictatorship	Cult of Personality
A dictator keeps power by outlawing competing political parties.	A small group or individual with control over the military also leads the government. Power is held through force.	A leader creates a perfect image of themselves. This convinces citizens that they are what is best for the country.

SilverTips for SUCCESS

★SilverTips for REVIEW

Review what you've learned. Use the text to help you.

Define key terms

autocracy
cult of personality
military dictatorship
one-party state
totalitarian

Check for understanding

What is an autocracy, and how is it related to a dictatorship?

Describe at least two ways a dictator can come to power.

Explain at least one method a dictator may use to remain in power.

Think deeper

How might your life be different if the style of government in your city, state, or nation changed?

★SilverTips for TAKING TESTS

- **Make a study plan.** Ask your teacher what the test is going to cover. Then, set aside time to study a little bit every day.
- **Read all the questions carefully.** Be sure you know what is being asked.
- **Skip any questions** you don't know how to answer right away. Mark them and come back later if you have time.

Glossary

autocracy a form of government ruled by one person with total power

citizens people who live in a particular country, city, or town

coup a sudden overthrowing of a government by a small group, often of the military

cult of personality a situation in which a public figure is presented as someone to be admired and loved

dynasty a group of rulers from the same family over a long period of time

monarchy a form of government with a single leader that has power passed between members of a family

propaganda often untrue or incomplete information that is spread to gain support for something

totalitarian relating to a political system in which the government has complete control over the people

Read More

Davis, Jane R. *Ten Terrible Conquerors (History's Very Worst).* Buffalo, NY: Gareth Stevens Publishing, 2026.

Faust, D. R. *Monarchy (Forms of Government: Need to Know).* Minneapolis: Bearport Publishing, 2026.

Kenney, Karen Latchana. *Checks and Balances (U.S. Government: Need to Know).* Minneapolis: Bearport Publishing, 2022.

Learn More Online

1. Go to **FactSurfer.com** or scan the QR code below.
2. Enter "**Dictatorship**" into the search box.
3. Click on the cover of this book to see a list of websites.

Index

About the Author

D. R. Faust is a freelance writer of fiction and nonfiction. They live in Queens, NY.